Between Thoughts

Poetry born from mindstorms

Prachi Wagh

BookLeaf Publishing

India | USA | UK

Made with ❤ on the BookLeaf Publishing Platform
www.bookleafpub.in
www.bookleafpub.com

Dedication

To

Nagesh, Kabir, Mira
Aai & Baba

for always providing food for thought.

Preface

Poetry is often personal. In that sense, one can't ever be sure what the reader makes of it. I know that all thoughts are not valid. The mind is a trickster, an illusionist. But only when you are lost, can you be found. When you are engulfed by darkness, light becomes a thing of beauty. Mindstorms spark ideas that instigate a further mental investigation. I feel compelled to catch these fleeting thoughts before they vanish. Most of my poetry simply gives shape, form and spelling to the thoughts that are caught between more 'important' thoughts. Turning seemingly pointless points into a point. Voicing the voices in my mind.

The poems are in no particular order. You can read from any page.

I hope this poetry serves as a bridge between chaos and clarity, making sense of the intangible.

Acknowledgements

I received the gift of language from my parents and my school Divine Child High School, Mumbai. Without these, poetry would not be possible for me.

Forever grateful to:

Ashwini Nande, my dear friend whose poetry inspired me in my teenage years.

Nagesh Wagh and Gauri Vipat who bear my banter with patience.

Nishanth Venkatesh and Seema Mehta for being among the first few to think my poetry was worth putting out in public.

Bookleaf Publishing for connecting poets, poetry and people. And Deepti Parikh for the thoughtful cover design.

1. Coffee Conversations

I sit with my coffee
and muddled thoughts
Why, How, When
What and whatnots

Rush, Overwhelm
a dark decoction
Quicksand sinking
begging action

Move frantic?
Deeper Ill sink
Struggle, strike
I'll be gone in a blink

"Stay," I say
Loosen the grip
Acknowledge the trap
and avoid the trip

I let the sand slip
out of my palm
I am still sinking
but I am calm

"Hello", I say
"You're not so bad"
To a nagging thought
that's labelled 'sad'

"Come sit with me
Ill hold your hand
until you can rise
shed your weight and stand"

And then I take another
and I do the same
I see it turn to vapour
before I give it a name

One by one I clear
the muddy puddle in my mind
As I sip the warm coffee
and leave an empty cup behind.

2. Shape of me

I am not going to fit myself in a box
Just so that I'm easy to carry around
I am not going to flow like shapeless water
To fill your cup and be glass bound.

My curves and sharp edges are as much me
As my ability to flatten out and fold up
I may bend because I love you
But if you challenge me Ill hold up.

So before we define the shape of me
Before we decree my degree
Let's agree,
That XS can be excess
And XL could excel
I don't need to confine or conform
I can shapeshift and I'll still be me.

3. Pillow Talk

On my pillow rest
restless thoughts

On my pillow lie lies
that tie me in knots

My pillow does not
soak sweet dreams
It is rather sour from dried tears
and bitter from silent screams

I dress it in fresh covers
but the insides are stale
from infinite repetitions
of a sordid old tale

Much truth hides
in its cotton thread
It knows exactly
whats going on in my head

My pillow is a folder
of unfinished drafts
My pillow is a holder

of imagined crafts

My pillow is witness
to forbidden desire
It won't betray me
it is a seasoned liar

My pillow knows so many secrets
I'd rather give you my arm
than share my pillow.

4. Love In Teacups

Two half cups of tea
One for you, one for me
Always half full, half empty
You finish yours and reach out for mine
Always needing one sip more.

You poke your fingers into my curved spine
to straighten my slouch when I am lost deep in a draft
I massage your shoulders as I pass your desk
and remind you to blink.

We zip out for a drive
because I love being driven
You agree even when you know
there will be a traffic jam.

I sense your irritation at the deadlock
and play your favourite song
Apologetically.

We don't exchange flowers
or buy grand gifts
But we remember to pack tea bags in lunch boxes
And keep the AC temperature at 27 degrees.

Who knows if we will grow old together or not
So while we are here and now
I try trekking and keeping up with cricket
While you try to show up for every Kathak concert.

We never fill our tea cups to the brim
even when we know
we need a little more
So we can reach out to each other
for that one last sip.

5. Hidden Corners

They are everywhere
these hidden corners.
When you tumble down memory lane
you carefully avoid that bend
and turn a blind eye
Because you know there lies a dark moment
One you don't want to remember.

In your home there is a place
Where you hide your private space
Where you can be yourself
When you are by yourself.

In the wardrobe
Behind all possessions
Tucked away is something
Truly your own.
Not for sharing, entirely your own.

They are everywhere
These hidden corners.
Under the sheets
Beyond the shelves
In that old jewellery box

we have hidden ourselves
An older version we no longer like
Or, no longer like to face.

In your heart, they exist as cold storage
Preserving the unsaid.
They hold on to words
that rise from your chest
but get caught in the throat.

In the folds of these pages
where ink flows fearless
and thoughts dance their wild dance
There are messages only I know exist.
Words in plain sight
Meanings in hidden corners.

6. Weight

Do you feel that weight?
The type that holds you back
like a chain of logs.
When you are ready to sprint
like jammed cogs.

That dead weight which makes you sink
just when you float to the surface.
The overarching mass of the wall you hit
just when you pick up pace.

That pot brimming over your head
freezing you to stay still.
That heavy silence so loaded
dare a secret spill.

The weight of tired shoulders
that won't even lift to shrug.
Arms hung limp with loss
they won't even return a hug.

Eyes so glazed they barely glance
at fleeting frames of a frenzied dance.
Tongue so tied in a silken knot

it won't let out a stifled thought.

That pit in your stomach
swallowing a vacuum
sucking all you know
into its heavy hollowness.
That hole in your heart
burying the burden of memories
so dark and bottomless.

That gravity at the summit
The load of longing
Weight of expectation
dangerously hanging.

Inertia and fatigue
from trying and failing.
The weight of an endless wait.
Do you feel the weight?

7. The Winter Inside

Warm blood gushing from the heart
clotting into icicles at my fingertips.

Breath like a haunting chill
Touch like a cold rock
Voice cracking like a dead tree branch
Eyes parched behind a frozen film of tears.

When soft moist thoughts fizzle and turn to ash
I know there is winter inside.

8. Sunsets

Crimson
Purple
Nearly Black
Not so dark yet
Not so stark.

Cooling sands
slipping through my hands
Flying strands
across my face
As I watch
the eternal grace.

My breath steadies
My heart readies
To say goodbye
As I soak in the sky
And watch the end of another day.

Then, there is something infinite
The beginning of an endless night
A feeling, a calling, a dread, a chill
A longing, a wait, a stirring so still.

A sky that shields
a foreboding that never yields
A restless rest
A heavy chest.

The colours blend
Just as memories do
Until it is hard to tell
the beginning from end.

Sunsets bring an uneasy calm
Like an ice cube melting away through my palm
A silence so loud so deep
An odd fear of falling asleep.

9. Winter Sunsets

In a city that has no winter
A breeze feels like a blessing
An absence of agenda and nothing next to 'next steps'
Is not a situation worth stressing.

Sweaty summers will come for sure
2025 dairies will soon be piling
But ill keep my window open this time
And write all that keeps me smiling
Not just what matters for filing.

Ill let empty spaces occupy places
Allow gaps in time, metre and rhyme
And when I sleep a sleep not so deep
Ill remember rare winter sunsets
And revel in nothingness sublime.

10. Drawing Lines

Drawing lines.
Tough isn't it?

Between passion and possession
Love and obsession.

Giving in or allowing?
Believing or knowing?

Perception and reality?
Stagnation and stability?

Getting wiser or ageing?
Ageing or maturing?

Mother or friend?
Parent or police?
Good cop and bad cop
Knowing when to stop.

Drawing lines is not my forte.
I am often lost
reading between the lines.

11. Solitude

By my window I discover
Many 'not so urgent' to dos

So many 'maybe tomorrow's
And some 'some day's

My seclusion and my solitude
Have never done me this good!

12

. Calendar Calling

It stares at me
like my math teacher from 7th grade
Who would tap her tow in waiting
And the numbers in my brain would fade

This thing- the calendar, its such a bully
I live my life to live up to it
Pleasing it with plans
Filling it fully

It seems too demanding
Always wanting more
Intolerant of gaps
Piling chore after chore

It looks down at me
Condescendingly
If there is ever a day
Even an hour that's free

It screams 'do something'
How come you aren't busy
If you are not exhausted

Shame on you 'Miss Lazy'.

So I've decided in 2025
I won't be keeping score
Instead, I'll live by the learnings
Of twenty twenty-four

So here goes I've made a list
I won't ramble I'll give you the gist

January, don't hurry
Dont let concern turn to worry

In February just chill
And learn to be still

In March no marching
Even if the world is overarching

April's rule- Be no fool!
The mind is not your master
The mind is just a tool

May may get hot
Be prepared to sweat a lot

But don't forget this tune

Breathe and hum through June

Dont hide from the cloudy sky
Soak in the joy of July

In August take your time
uncertainty is fine

Focus on 'process', remember
Savour the slow in September

Be present stay sober
No overthinking in October

Acknowledge the now in November
Dare to detach in December

Tell the calendar- Take a walk
Tell the calendar- Not to stalk

Let the clock tick
Let the pages turn
Just be the light
While the candles burn

Ignore the calendar and you'll see
you'll soon stop becoming

And finally, you'll be.

21

13. Retelling an untold tale

Once upon a time
In the heart of this land
Lived a woman whose heart
Was as gentle as her hand

She cooked and she cleaned
Kept a tidy house
She loved her dear husband
Who wasn't a bad spouse

She checked all the boxes
Of being a good bride
Little did she know
She had something inside!

Imprisoned within her
Were a story and a song
A tale she never told
A song unsung for long

The story suffocated
The song began to choke
Release! That is what they needed
So finally the spell broke

Out came the story
As the woman slept one day
Free to talk to tell
Free to run away

The story escaped
Full of news and views
Disguising itself
Into a man's shoes

The song snuck out
and hummed about
Sweet notes afloat
tuned into a coat

Her man came home
As evening fell
"Who's in the house?
Woman pray tell!"

"No one" she she said clueless
Wondering how it could be
A strange coat and shoes
But whose she could not see

"Liar! You cheat"

The man began to blame
"How dare you" she cried
As she lit the lamp flame

The woman wept to sleep
Heartbroken by his doubt
Suspicious, jealous, furious
The husband stormed out

Now all the lamp flames in town
Once they were put out
Would assemble in the temple
They had much to gossip about
The houses they came from
The wives, husbands and lovers
Things that happened in daylight
Secrets that played under covers

"Why so late" they asked
The latecomer that night
"Oh my man and lady
You had to hear them fight!"

She told them of the story and song
That her lady had done nothing wrong
"She didn't even know they were within her
Buried so deep she didn't remember"

The husband lay in the temple
Nowhere to sleep so there he went
Hearing the flames gossip
The man began to repent

Guilty, he went home at dawn
And asked his wife about her story and song
"Tell me what tale you know
Sing the song, let it flow"

She stared at him and then away
What could she sing what could she say
Bottled in too long, withered and rotten
The tune the tale were long forgotten.

The song she never sang
The tale she never told
What she had within had left
The truth would never unfold.

-An Indian folktale

14. Wrinkles

The wrinkles at the corner of your eye
are like folds of an old mulmul blanket
that becomes softer with each passing year.

The sprinkle of residual mischief
that you now wisely withhold
hides in the deep crescent drawn by your smile.

I melt watching your restraint
The calm acceptance of life and age
The poise and the push ever so gentle
The easy transition into every new stage.

15. The Dancing Body

Like rising vapour drifting away
Like fingers tracing curves on a dusty surface
I urge to move, to emerge, to melt
To go as far as the mind can go
To reach within the layers of the heart
To unravel the wrapped
To utter the unsaid
To touch the intangible
To be that one cannot be.

16. Unforgotten

Our Miraj home and its stone 'katta'
Summers spent under the lemon tree
Plucking flowers for Aji's pooja and gajra
Dada's amti-poli and and ancient bicycle.

Weeks without TV or telephone
Just us and our time
to do as we please
Mind you, not just laze at ease.

Morning walks a.k.a temple hopping
Playing pretend
on the swing, in the passage, on the steps
Setting up home or shop
across the house and the yard
in our imaginary city.

Cooking up stories
about what hides inside the locked shed
Discovering treasure or a treasure map.

Star gazing to the sounds of the neighbour's TV
Sleeping across the living room on neat rows of
mattresses.

Never a dull moment, never bored.

Simply being in Miraj
is a childhood unforgotten.

17. Fear

He was gone
I grew up strong
I believed that lie
But he never really left me
After he left.

He lingered on
Under my skin
Grew with me
Or didn't let me grow?
Now I want to know
Is it him?
Or is it just me?

I tear a page
I shed a tear
I bite my lip
I show my fear.

My eyes hurry
My brow flickers
I wondered if this is me
Is it I who wonders?

18. Hurt

It stings
It throbs
It raises it's ugly head
It steals It robs
It always gets ahead.

It hides in places
You have long forgotten
It shows up
Gate crashes
Feels fresh though rotten.

It plays dead
like a dormant volcano
and comes back
like incarnates.
Hurt never heals
it only hibernates.

19. Love Is

Love is
knowing that when he holds me
he doesn't hold me back
Knowing that he will know
when to love is to let go.

20. Setting Free

Letting go
Ego
Letting disappear
Fear
Letting retire
Desire
Letting be
Me.

21. Release

Show me the tears
You hid in the rain
That spot in plain sight
Where you hide your pain

That chamber of screams
Where you empty your heart
That tattered notebook
Now falling apart

Let out that breath
You've held for so long
Let the unfinished verse
Turn into song

Show me the hand
You slid in your pocket to stop it from shaking
Show me that piggy bank of worries
On the verge of breaking

Spit out that venom
brewing in your throat
Throw out the baggage
that's sinking your boat

Tell me that dream
That keeps you from sleeping
Shake off the daze
That keeps you from dreaming

Reveal your cracks
Flaunt your flaws
Break rules that gag you
To hell with those laws

Say you are stuck
Say you are lost
Ask for help
Don't count the cost.

You don't need to bleed until you clot
Let me be the solace you sought.

22. Anti Aging

Some day
Ill behold the beauty of the bulge on my belly
The lazy languid linger in my lonely limping gait
The fluidity of my frequently fluctuating weight.

Ill be ok
With forgetting names and promises
And make peace with unruly unpredictable curls
That seem to have a mind of their own
Even as they wrap the fickle mind underneath.

And ill cherish
This fickle mind with its flaws
Like the missing teeth from my jaws
The bend in my back and the blur in my eyes.

I'll look kindly
At my sagging skin
And reimagine all that it holds within its folds.

All this I'll accept
And smile at myself with wonder and pride
Some day, one day.

Until then, I lose to my vanity. And denial.

37

23. And Finally

I've reached a point
where I see the pointlessness of it all.
No matter matters.
What I did
Do
Or Will do.
Yet I wake up
to keep doing
the doing
that will never be done.
Reached that point
that points to the pointlessness of it all.